C0-AZU-207

TIME LIFE BOOKS **Your Money Matters**

Credit

Basics

By Marc Robinson

Alexandria, Virginia

State Street Global Advisors: educating people about money
For 200 years, we have been in the banking business helping people manage and invest their money. We are a global leader in the investment management industry, serving institutions and individuals worldwide.

Our goal in creating this series is to give you unbiased, useful information that will help you manage your money. No product advertisements. No sales pitches. Just straightforward, understandable information.

Our ultimate hope is that after reading these books you feel more informed, more in control of your money, and perhaps most importantly, more able to successfully plan and reach your financial goals.

Time-Life Books is a division of
TIME LIFE INCORPORATED

Time-Life Custom Publishing
Vice President and Publisher: Terry Newell
Director of Sales: Neil Levin
Director, New Business Development: Phyllis A. Gardner
Senior Art Director: Christopher M. Register
Managing Editor: Donia Ann Steele
Production Manager: Carolyn Bounds
Quality Assurance Manager: James D. King

Second Printing. PRINTED IN U.S.A.

Robinson, Marc, 1955-
Credit basics : it's just what you need to know / by Marc Robinson.
p. cm. – (Time Life Books your money matters)
ISBN 0-7835-4794-3
1. Credit. I. Title II. Series.
HG3701.R63 1996
332.7'43 - - dc20 96-20267
CIP

For State Street Global Advisors,
The Lab:
Clark Kellogg
Jenny Phillips
Sally Nellson
Paul Schwartz

For Top Down:
Marc Robinson
Mark Shepherd

Design: Adams/Morioka, Inc.

TABLE OF

Contents

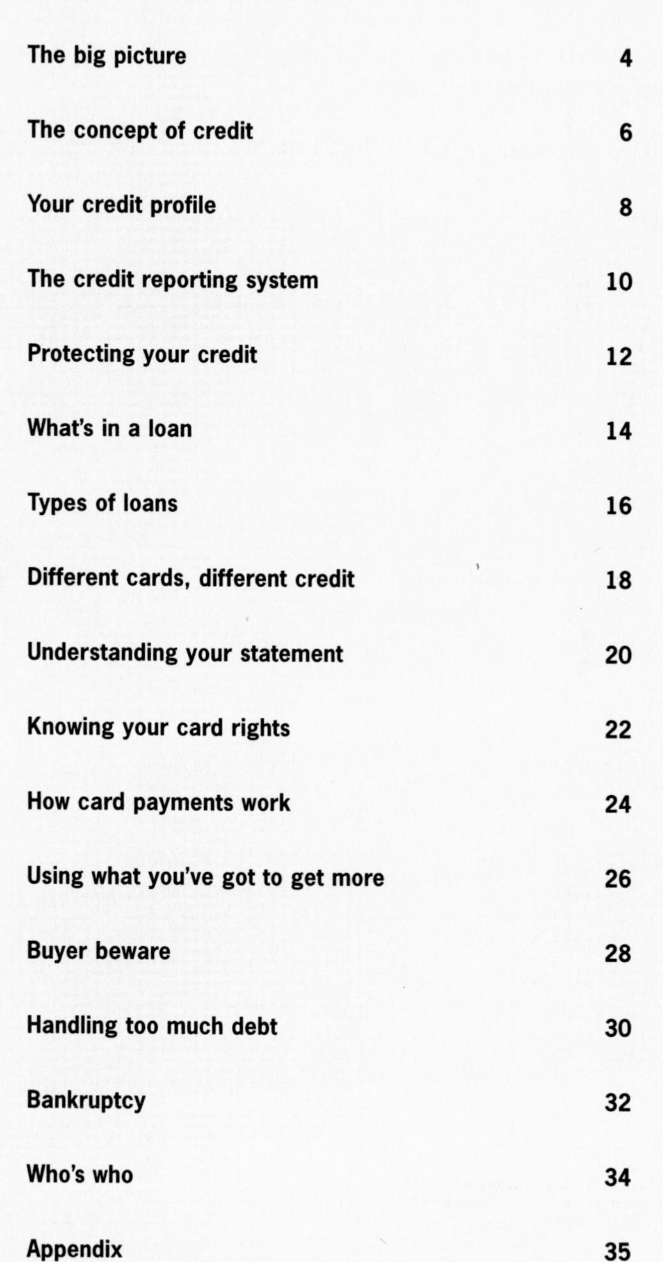

The big picture

The credit world is a never-ending cycle of borrowing and lending money people don't have but expect to have in the future. Because of the credit system, our society has a lot more "buying power" than "cash." As long as you faithfully repay what you borrow, you'll allow your lender to faithfully repay what he or she borrowed, which will allow the lender's lender to do the same, and so on. It's a delicate system: Each time someone breaks a promise or loses faith in someone else, the system suffers because

the entire system is based on trust and credibility.

1. **Buyers** (businesses and people like you) often want a product or service that costs more than they're willing or able to pay with cash. So, they find a lender (such as a credit card issuer or bank), or ask the seller to arrange a loan for them (as is common in car purchases).

2. **Sellers** (e.g., store owners, service providers) need to make sales to stay in business. Therefore, some offer loans to customers. Others arrange for their customers to get a loan from an outside lender (and take a commission for arranging the deal). Still others allow third parties (e.g., credit card issuers) to "front" the money for buyers. In any case, at the time of the sale, little or no cash changes hands, but the sellers can record a sale *and* lenders can record new loans.

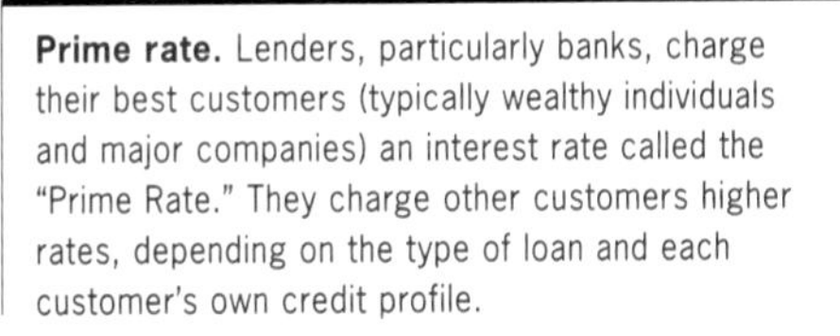

Prime rate. Lenders, particularly banks, charge their best customers (typically wealthy individuals and major companies) an interest rate called the "Prime Rate." They charge other customers higher rates, depending on the type of loan and each customer's own credit profile.

Discount rate. This is the interest rate that the Federal Reserve Bank charges banks. It's always lower than the Prime Rate so that banks are assured of borrowing at a lower rate and lending at a higher rate.

Playing by different rules. People who repay faithfully and don't "overextend" themselves will build better credit and make it easier to borrow again. The Federal Reserve, however, is different. It can borrow as much as it wants because it's backed by a guarantee to all lenders called the "full faith and credit" of the federal government. In other words, we're asked to have complete faith in the government's credit that it will repay what we lend.

5. Businesses and individuals (like you) lend money to the government every time it auctions Treasury bonds. (When you buy a "bond," you are actually lending the bond issuer money and expecting to be repaid on a schedule with interest.) The government adds an incentive: The interest is exempt from state income taxes. This means you may actually earn interest from loans you made to the government (for example, through Treasury bonds), and use that money to help repay money you may have borrowed.

4. The federal government's bank, called the Federal Reserve Bank, lends money to banks specifically to supply them with enough cash to stay in business. The "Fed" makes the loans based on their trust that the banks will repay faithfully (which partly depends on the bank's borrowers—like you—repaying them faithfully). The Fed, however, must also get money from somewhere. They can print more, get it from taxes, and borrow it.

3. Lenders make loans based on the trust that their borrowers will repay faithfully. Then they need to raise more cash to be able to make more loans and stay in business. So, lenders also borrow money from other lenders, and if they're a bank, they can also borrow directly from the federal government.

The concept of credit

When people offer you credit, they're saying, "I believe you'll repay me." In fact, "credit" comes from the Latin word "credo," which means "I believe." As our society moves further away from paper money and coins, your daily finances become more dependent on the trust people have in you. The credit system is open to all. If you choose to use credit with good judgment, its power will increase with use. If you misuse it, the power will decrease. Like anything based on people's faith in each other, credit

is both a fragile and a precious thing.

You're offered it

Actually, credit is difficult to avoid. The moment you ask for electricity in your home, you'll enter the credit system. Since the utility can't know in advance how much you'll use, they let you use their product daily but pay them only once a month. (The utility may, however, ask you for a security deposit.)

Many stores and dealers of every kind will also encourage you to buy on credit even if you can afford to pay cash. It's seen as a way to establish a comfortable relationship with customers and to make it easy for you to buy more of their products.

People who own homes are familiar with credit: They've received a mortgage loan. In fact, the government entices all of us to use this form of credit by offering the single biggest tax break—tax deductions on mortgage loan interest payments.

You use it or store it

To use the credit that's offered, you simply buy now and agree to pay later: You borrow. There can be significant benefits.

- Rather than wait to save up so you can afford something, you can use it while you pay for it. And with a credit card, you can purchase goods by phone from almost anywhere in the world.

- You could also choose to save your credit for when you really need it rather than use it right away. This is called having "buying power." For example, you have instant access to cash in an emergency. It also gives you the flexibility to buy on the spur of the moment, beat a price increase, or take advantage of a sale.

You repay your debt

When you borrow money, you "go into debt," and are required to repay what you borrow. Those payments will claim a portion of your future income but will also reduce your debt. By spreading payments over time and paying interest, you'll increase the overall cost of borrowing. But that may be offset by two advantages: avoiding a lump sum payment up front and being able to budget for the future.

Whenever you accept credit, you must sign a credit agreement. Once you signify that you've read and understood it, you'll be bound by its terms and conditions.

You build more credit

Your performance in repaying the debt, showing how you handle credit, is reported by the lender to the credit bureau. If you've repaid faithfully and handled any problems conscientiously, you'll most likely be offered more credit. Every time you borrow and repay—every time you use your credit—the cycle begins again. Each time the cycle is completed, your ability to borrow will either increase or decrease depending on your performance. It's your responsibility to ensure that your ability to repay matches your ability to borrow.

If you neglect to make timely repayments, you break your contract. If the lender seeks legal recourse, future credit will be difficult for you to obtain.

Your credit profile

Credit is highly personal because it's a reflection of you. Your credit profile doesn't make you a good or bad person, but it does make you a good or bad credit risk. It's a snapshot of both financial and personal integrity because offering credit is an expression of trust in you to repay as agreed. Remember, though: Lenders want to extend you credit because that's how they make money. They'll change their "yes" to "no" only if they consider you too risky. In most cases,

you present yourself using two documents.

The application

You fill this out to ask for credit. Lenders typically assess these criteria:

1. Character. Part of trusting that you'll repay what you borrow depends on your stability as a person and an income-earner. For example, someone who often changes homes or jobs may have a less settled, less reliable personality—or may be hard to find should the lender have problems with repayment. These are two of the reasons you're asked to list all your addresses and employers over the past three to five years.

2. Ability to repay. In a nutshell, can you afford to repay what you borrow? Your job history provides insights into your earning potential, including how much you've earned, whether there's been a steady increase, and of course, the amount you're currently earning.

Your assets also yield insights. Do you own a home (which also speaks to your stability)? Do you have investments (which shows you can save money)?

Finally, there's the load you're already carrying or could carry: What debts do you currently owe? And how much credit is already available to you (through cards and other lines of credit)? In other words, are you now, or could you possibly ever become, overextended?

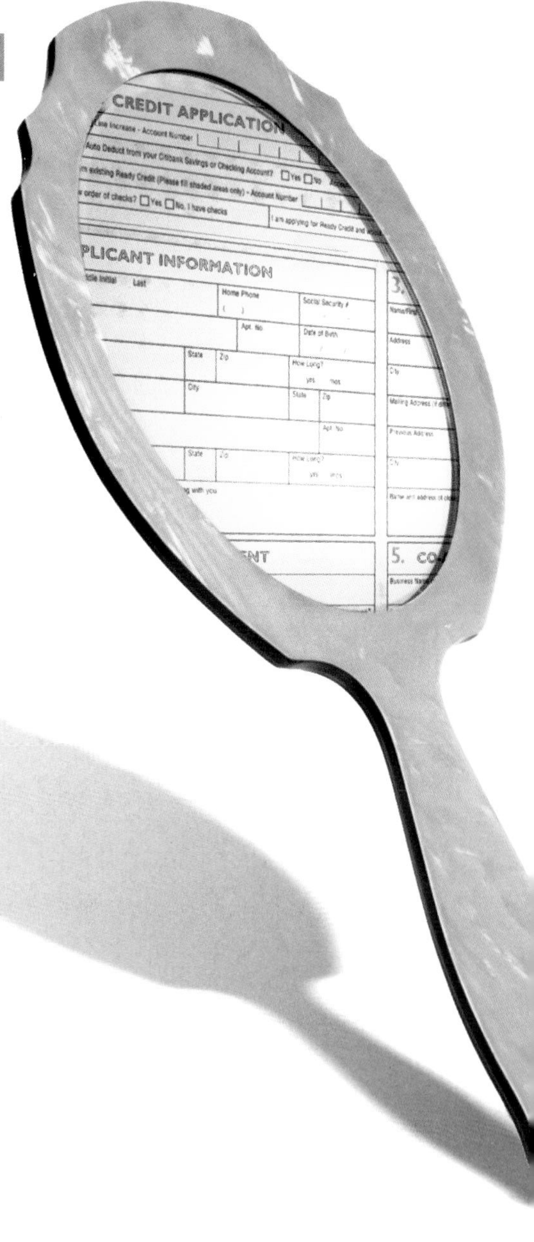

The credit report

This report verifies the truth of what you put on your application and presents your actions and attitudes toward credit (your "creditworthiness"). It lists the amount of credit that has been made available to you and details your borrowing and repaying habits. In other words, it shows how you treat credit *and* your relationships with creditors.

What's not in a report. There's nothing about race, religion, sexual preference, medical history, criminal records, or political preferences.

Each report contains:

Personal information. Your full name, nicknames, current and previous addresses, employers, birth date, and social security number.

Matters of public record. Any relevant court records, such as legal judgments, tax liens, bankruptcies, or overdue child support.

Credit history. A snapshot of your past actions. How faithfully have you repaid other creditors? The report lists all loans and credit lines in your name from recent years. Reports vary from bureau to bureau, but generally they show the type of loan, the date you began the loan or opened the credit line, the amount of the loan or credit limit, the amount you still owe, and your payment pattern. For example, the report may list the number of times you've paid late, including the times you were more than 30, 60, and 90 days late.

Inquiries. A list of who has received a report within the past two years (by law, though, a bureau is only required to show inquiries made within the past six months). It's common for a potential lender to turn you down because of "excessive inquiries." Right or wrong, the thinking is that many inquiries could indicate that you're asking many lenders for credit—a situation that could lead to you becoming overextended (and unable to repay the lender reviewing your report).

The credit reporting system

It's possible that every time you apply for credit, use your credit, repay what you borrowed, or don't repay, your activity is recorded, communicated, collated, and stored in the data banks of a national credit reporting system. This system is crucial to both borrowers and lenders. Since most lenders don't personally know their borrowers, they depend on the bureaus to provide reliable, independent verification of your creditworthiness. And with the aid of computer technology, many credit checks can now occur in an instant.

Here is how it works.

Information goes in

When you put in an application. Every time you apply for employment, insurance, or credit, you give someone permission to receive a credit report on you. Inquiries are usually directed to one or more of the three national credit bureaus. The inquiry itself becomes useful information (because it's a credit-related activity) and will appear on any subsequent report for at least six months—and usually two years.

When businesses send in reports. Typically, any business that extends you credit or sells you insurance also sends the bureaus a monthly update on how well you (and their other customers) are keeping up the payments. It's an imperfect system. Not all businesses send reports regularly, and some don't send reports to all the national credit bureaus.

Public records. Any tax lien, bankruptcy, court judgment, or other legal event that has an impact on your future ability to repay—or the perception of your willingness to repay—goes into your file.

National credit bureaus. Credit reporting bureaus collect information, collate it, and keep everything in their vast computer databases. There is no actual "report" stored on you. Instead, when there's an inquiry, the bureau draws all of your data from the computer and creates the report.

Just the facts. The reporting system is essentially impartial and nonjudgmental. Reports show facts about your credit history. Some bureaus, however, also provide business customers with "risk scores" (and leave them out of reports sent to you). These scores are based on the facts in your report and indicate, among other things, the likelihood of your going into bankruptcy or of paying chronically late.

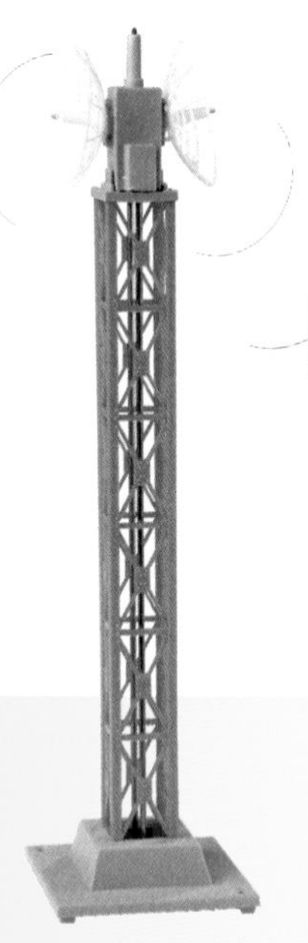

Reports go out

Under the Fair Credit Reporting Act, no one can see your report except you or someone to whom you've given written permission (in an application, for example).

Although all three national bureaus share information, they're still in competition for customers: Businesses pay to be members so they can have the right to order credit reports. Bureaus are very stringent about the legitimacy of their members, and the law is also strict on privacy. Anyone who obtains a credit report under false pretenses may be fined and jailed.

The Equal Credit Opportunity Act protects all consumers against decisions based on personal biases by restricting what bureaus can report. They can't reveal race, religion, or criminal records, but they can reveal court judgments since those could affect your ability to repay.

In the end, your application for credit is either approved or rejected based on the lender's assessment of your creditworthiness. A rejection won't be reported or appear on a later credit report.

The "Big Three" bureaus that control the national reporting system are:

- Equifax Credit Information Services
- Trans Union Corporation
- TRW Information Services

Since each bureau may have different information, you may have three credit histories, not one.

Local credit bureaus. There are several thousand local bureaus. Most receive their data from the three national bureaus, although they may have more local credit information on you in their databases.

Protecting your credit

Your credit report isn't always an accurate reflection of your credit activities. With millions of data entries coming and going between merchants and credit bureaus every day, there are bound to be errors and misunderstandings. Of course, your report may be accurate but still not be as positive as you'd wish. There are ways you can clean up your report. It's up to you, though; no one cares about your credit as much as you, and no one else can give you the ability

to get to the money you need when you need it.

Monitoring your reports

You're entitled to see your credit report at any time. TRW allows one free report per year. In 1996, Trans Union and Equifax charged a fee between $8 and $16 per report.

If you've been turned down. You're entitled to a free report from the credit bureau if something in your report has led to your being denied credit, a job, or insurance. By law, the company rejecting you has to send you written notice if one of the reasons for the decision was negative information on your credit report. You must request your report within 30 days of this written notice.

To request a report (free or otherwise), provide in writing your name, addresses from the past five years, social security number, birth date, phone number, and if applicable, a copy of the letter informing you that you were rejected because of the report.

Legal protection. You can sue anyone who obtains a report on you illegally or for illegal purposes. As of April 1996, the maximum you could collect was $2,500.

Fixing errors

Inaccurate credit reports are a common source of consumer complaints to the Federal Trade Commission. Although the three national credit bureaus try to resolve problems within 30 days, there's no guarantee they will. Make copies of everything you send them in case your letters are lost.

How it works. Every credit report comes with instructions on how to report errors. Follow them and return your request to the credit bureau. The bureau is supposed to contact the merchant who supplied the disputed information and ask if it's correct. If it's wrong, the bureau fixes your report. If the merchant doesn't answer within 90 days, the bureau is supposed to drop the information from the report (but you'll have to follow up to be sure). If the merchant says it's correct, the bureau will tell you.

Addresses and phones

You can mail requests for credit reports to the three national credit bureaus:

Equifax Information Service Center
PO Box 105873, Atlanta GA 30348.
Or fax to (404) 612-2668

Trans Union Customer Relations Center
PO Box 390, Springfield, PA 19064

TRW, Attention: NCAC, Box 9409, Allen, TX 75002

You can request a report by voice mail if you've been denied credit within the last 30 days. (If the phone request gets lost and you wait more than 30 days, you may be asked to pay for the report. To avoid confusion, mention the date of your phone request in your letter.)

Equifax: (800) 685-1111
Trans Union: (800) 851-2674
TRW: (800) 392-1122

Having your own say

By law, you can have the credit bureau place a statement—100 words maximum—in your file explaining your version of the dispute. The bureau must also include your statement in any report it sends out.

When you apply for a loan, a lender will see the statement and take it into account. You may also want to place a statement in your file to explain a period of delinquency caused by some unexpected event, such as serious illness or unemployment, that drastically reduced your income.

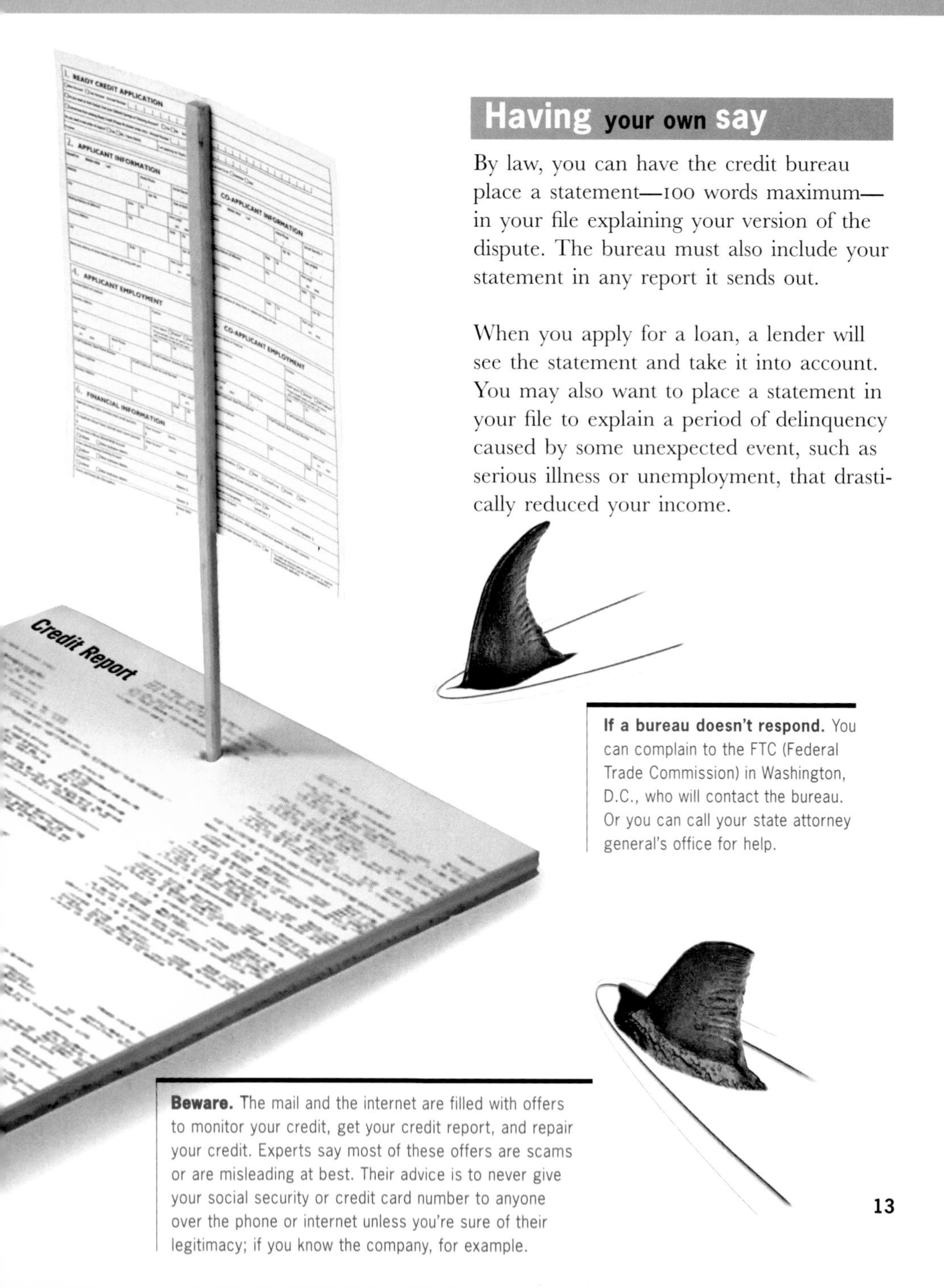

If a bureau doesn't respond. You can complain to the FTC (Federal Trade Commission) in Washington, D.C., who will contact the bureau. Or you can call your state attorney general's office for help.

Beware. The mail and the internet are filled with offers to monitor your credit, get your credit report, and repair your credit. Experts say most of these offers are scams or are misleading at best. Their advice is to never give your social security or credit card number to anyone over the phone or internet unless you're sure of their legitimacy; if you know the company, for example.

What's in a loan

The reason for having credit is to get a loan when you need it. A loan can be large or small; it can be instantly available through a card or it can require your signing a complicated set of documents. And although different kinds of loans come with different terms, virtually every credit agreement covers

four key points:

How much you can borrow

The amount you borrow is called the "principal." Sometimes you borrow the principal all at once. Other times, with credit cards for example, you have a "line of credit" that lets you borrow up to your "credit limit" at any time.

With credit cards and charge cards (where you pay in full each month and aren't charged interest), any principal you repay becomes available to be borrowed again—as long as your credit remains in good standing. This agreement to let you borrow, repay, and borrow again is called "revolving credit."

In a loan document and on most card statements, you may see the words "amount financed." It simply means the amount you borrowed.

How much it will cost

The most common cost of a loan is the interest (sometimes called a "finance charge"). Usually, your payments are split—part goes to repay what you borrowed and part goes to pay the interest.

There may also be fees of various kinds. Many card issuers charge annual fees (similar to dues) that they sometimes waive for special promotions or upon request. Many also charge fees for cash advances. Lenders of mortgages usually charge up-front interest called "points" and other, connected fees for appraisals, closing costs, and more.

Every lender is required to show you the annual percentage rate (APR). It takes into account the interest plus certain fees to show the actual cost of the loan for the first year.

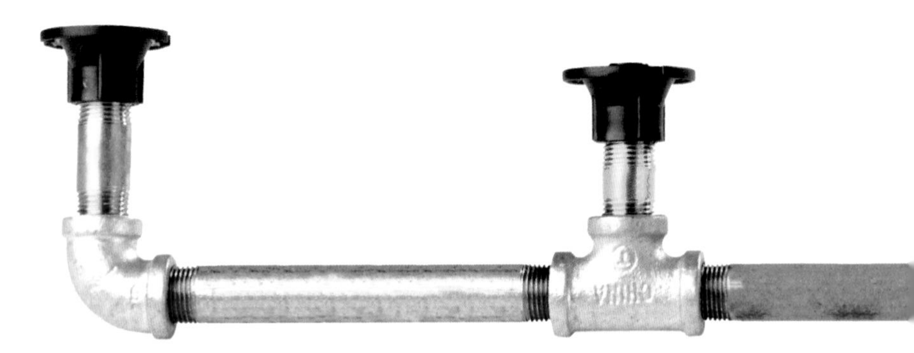

Limits on security. By law, creditors can't ask you to pledge as security any clothes, furniture, or other personal belongings unless they're the actual items you're buying on credit. Also, if your car is repossessed, you're entitled to anything left in it (although you may only have this right if you call within 24 hours).

The payment plan

A payment plan has three parts: the length of time you're given to repay the loan, the schedule of payments, and the amount of each payment.

Charge card issuers give you the shortest time—30 or 60 days. Mortgage lenders give you the longest—up to 30 years. Credit card issuers let you take as long as you like, if you always make the minimum payment required.

Although there are many different repayment schedules, the most common is once a month. Your payment amounts may be "fixed" (stay the same each time) or "adjustable" (change according to a formula at periodic intervals).

What if you don't repay

Failing to repay on schedule can put you in default. The lender is then faced with finding another way to be repaid. If your credit report shows you to be a risk, the lender will want "security." In a secured loan, you give the lender the right to sell specific property (called the "collateral") if you default. In this way, you give the lender a sense of security, which makes it easier for him or her to say "yes" to the loan.

Usually, the collateral is the property you're buying with the loan, such as a car, home, or large household item. But lenders can also ask borrowers to pledge an unrelated item of value. (The item chosen is negotiable, and you have to weigh the risk of losing that item against your need for the loan. The law also protects you from being forced to pledge certain necessities.)

Types of loans

In theory, virtually anyone can lend you money, from an uncle or employer to financial companies. In practice, you could get a better deal if your choice of lender is

based on your reason for wanting the money.

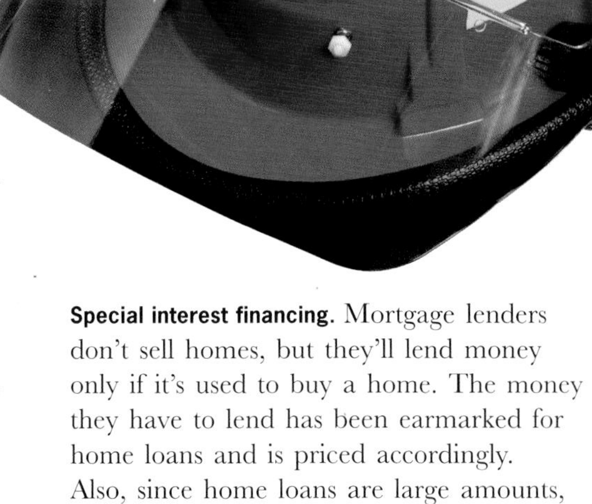

For a specific purpose

Some lenders will extend credit only if you'll use the money in ways that further their business. To them, the top consideration may be the purpose of the loan; second, whether you're pledging the purchased product as security to protect them; and third, the quality of your credit rating.

Seller financing. To make selling their products easier, many department stores, retail chains, and car dealerships serve as middlemen for lines of credit just as they do for the products they sell. They don't lend you the money to buy their products; they arrange loans from other lenders. For example, a store or car dealer may get you a loan from a finance company and receive a commission for the deal. In effect, they sell you a product, then sell you a loan to pay for that product.

You often have to pledge the property you're buying as security, in case you fail to repay the loan. The finance company legally owns the product (e.g., your car) until you repay the loan, and it has the right to repossess if you fail to make payments on time.

Special interest financing. Mortgage lenders don't sell homes, but they'll lend money only if it's used to buy a home. The money they have to lend has been earmarked for home loans and is priced accordingly. Also, since home loans are large amounts, lenders need to have a security interest in property of equal or greater value: namely, your home.

Lenders of student loans also insist you use the money for this specific purpose. Since you're buying an education, however, there's no tangible property for you to pledge as security. That's why many student loans are government guaranteed to encourage banks to lend.

Mutual support. Some retailers and lenders are owned by the same, larger company (e.g., Sears and General Motors), and support each other. For example, if the retailer needs to boost sales, the finance company may offer low-cost loans "for a limited time only." In any case, financing your purchase through the retailer means the larger company earns you as a customer twice; once for the product, and again for the loan.

Credit unions. A non profit alternative to banks, credit unions are run for and by their members. Some are open to the public but most are sponsored by an employer, association, university, or government, and are open only to members or employees and their families. Loans are made from money deposited by members. Generally, rates are lower than for bank loans.

Private finance companies. Often open to lending to people with poor credit records, these companies offset the increased risk by charging much higher rates. In other words, one of the downsides of having poor credit is you have to be willing to pay a lot more for a loan in order to convince someone to lend you money. (The companies—and the terms they offer—can range from reputable to very questionable.)

For any purpose

Some lenders extend credit without requiring you to specify how you'll use the money. Their first consideration is whether you're pledging an asset as security; second, the quality of your credit rating; and third (if considered at all), your purpose for the loan. Here are some examples:

Asset-based loan. A bank, securities broker, or insurance company may let you borrow against the value of your insurance, home, or investments if your property has enough value. Typically, these loans have lower interest rates than conventional loans. The lender reasons that if you own these assets, you've already exhibited financial responsibility and credibility. You're also protecting the lender by pledging assets of sufficient value to cover the loan in case you default.

Line of credit. This type of loan is a very useful tool in today's world although it's tempting to use it indiscriminately. You're given a credit limit (a maximum amount you can borrow). Then you're free to borrow up to that limit at any time for any purpose. Credit cards are the most common example, but home equity loans can also be lines of credit. Many banks offer lines of credit and use your checking or savings account as security.

Personal loan. You may get a loan on the strength of your name, or be asked to pledge an asset as security.

Pawning. Pawnbrokers lend money to anyone without checking credit. You bring in something of value, the broker lends you a small percentage of the item's value and holds the item for an agreed period of time. You can pay off the loan within that time and reclaim your property, but if you don't, the broker can sell it. Interest on these loans tends to be high. You may also have to pay for insurance and storage.

Different cards, different credit

Essentially, a card is an authorization—proof that someone has given you credit. By using a card, you tell a seller, "This financial institution has authorized me to buy your product without cash and has guaranteed your payment." The seller then contacts an agent of the card issuer to verify that you still have an account in good standing, and asks you to sign a receipt for the item. The kind of card you carry, therefore,

shows the credit you've requested and received.

Repay at your own pace

The most popular form of credit is an open line you can tap into—and repay—at your own pace (as long as you make at least the minimum payment required). It can take two forms:

Unsecured revolving credit. For this type of credit, you get a "credit card." There's a maximum you can borrow, and any amount you repay is immediately available to borrow again. You may pay interest on what you borrow or you may be given a period of time to repay in full without interest. Most credit cards are "unsecured," which means the lender isn't entitled to take specific property if you don't repay.

Secured revolving credit. People with poor credit or no credit history can usually receive a secured credit card through MasterCard or Visa. (Some retailers also offer secured cards.) It looks and works like any credit card, with this main difference: You have to keep money in a savings account (as "security") and allow the card issuer to tap into it if you fail to pay your bills. The amount of credit you receive is usually linked to the amount you deposit.

Co-branding. You can get a credit card (typically Visa or MasterCard) that offers promotional tie-ins from other companies. Every time you use the card, for example, the company (e.g., an airline or a car maker) awards you points you can then use to buy their products at a discount or get them for free. Read the terms carefully; some promotions are better than others.

Other benefits. Depending on who offers you credit and the level of credit you receive (e.g., a basic card or a gold card), you might receive added benefits such as:

- guaranteed hotel reservations
- double the manufacturer's warranty and extended service agreements on most products
- free collision coverage on auto rentals (no need to buy the agency's coverage)
- travel and emergency assistance, including medical and legal referrals when traveling and arranging emergency transportation to hospitals
- assistance with replacing lost tickets or luggage
- language interpreters
- delivery assistance for prescriptions, emergency cash, replacement for lost or stolen cards or valuable documents
- trip assistance, from ATM locations to weather reports and health and legal requirements in your destination

To find out your benefits, read the brochure that comes with your card or call the customer service number on the back of the card.

Repay in full each time

Travel and entertainment cards (also called "charge" cards) show that you've been extended credit, but only for short terms: You're required to pay in full by the due date for any item that appears on your statement. There are, however, no interest charges. American Express (which allows you 30 days to pay) and Diners Club (which allows you 60 days to pay) are the two most famous issuers of this credit.

Rebates. Some card issuers promote rebates on purchases. Look at these closely. For example, in one promotion a card issuer offered a 1% rebate—on a year's worth of finance charges, not purchases. So, if you spent $15,000 on the card in a year and paid, for example, $275 in interest that year, you'd receive a $2.75 rebate.

Pay as you go

You can also get a debit card, which doesn't technically give you credit. Instead, every time you use it your bank takes the money from your account ("debits") and sends it directly to the merchant. If the money isn't in your account, the transaction will be rejected. ATM cards (the cards used to do banking at "automated teller machines") are the most popular debit cards.

Debit cards don't offer as much protection against fraud or billing disputes as credit and charge cards. For one thing, it's harder to recover money already paid from your account.

The PIN (personal identification number). To use your card for cash advances or withdrawals, you'll need to create a PIN (a password). Protect your PIN very carefully. Don't write it down, tell it to anyone, or let it be overheard.

Understanding your statement

Your statement is a snapshot of your account. Most of all, it tells you three things: how much you owed to start the period, how much you owed at the end of the period (on the date the statement was printed, called the "closing date"), and the transactions that got you from start to end. Formats vary but generally each statement includes the information shown here. Reading your statement is the best way

to track spending, monitor charges, and catch errors.

What you'll see

This explains what your credit has cost you this past period and how the cost was calculated. This information doesn't exist for cards such as Diners Club and American Express, because they don't charge interest.

Previous balance. What you owed on the day the last statement (not this one) was printed.

Purchases. What you bought during this statement period.

Payments. The amount you repaid and that was, therefore, reinstated to your credit line.

Credits. The total amount, if any, credited to your account because you overpaid, a charge was in error, or you returned merchandise.

Finance charge. The amount of interest charged this period. For example, if you're charged 1.5125% every period on the balance you owe, the annual percentage rate (APR) comes to 18.15% a year. For cash advances, you also pay 18.15% but you are charged interest from the day you receive the advance. (You're also charged a fee, typically 2% of the advance with a minimum of $2.50.)

Late charges. The penalty for paying after the due date.

Minimum amount due. The least you're required to pay before the due date.

Payment due date. The date by which the card issuer must receive your payment if you want to avoid a late charge.

Average daily balance. Each day, the card issuer calculates a new balance by adding new purchases and fees and subtracting any payments and credits. At the end of the month, the total of these daily balances is divided by the number of days in the period. You're then charged interest based on that average amount.

Over the limit. Some issuers let you go over your credit limit by 10% or so; others consider an extra dollar to be a violation.

The status of your account

This summarizes your borrowing power.

Closing date (also called "billing date"). The last day of the period. Charges and payments after this date appear on your next statement.

Credit line (also called "credit limit"). The most you can borrow. If you try to go over, a store will probably be told to refuse the card. If you have a good payment record, you can ask to raise your limit.

Cash advance limit. The most you can borrow in cash. Not all card issuers put a limit on cash advances.

New balance. The amount you owed on the day the statement was printed.

Available credit line. What you could've borrowed on the day the statement was printed. (The credit line minus the new balance.)

Available cash limit. The most cash you could have borrowed on the day the statement was printed.

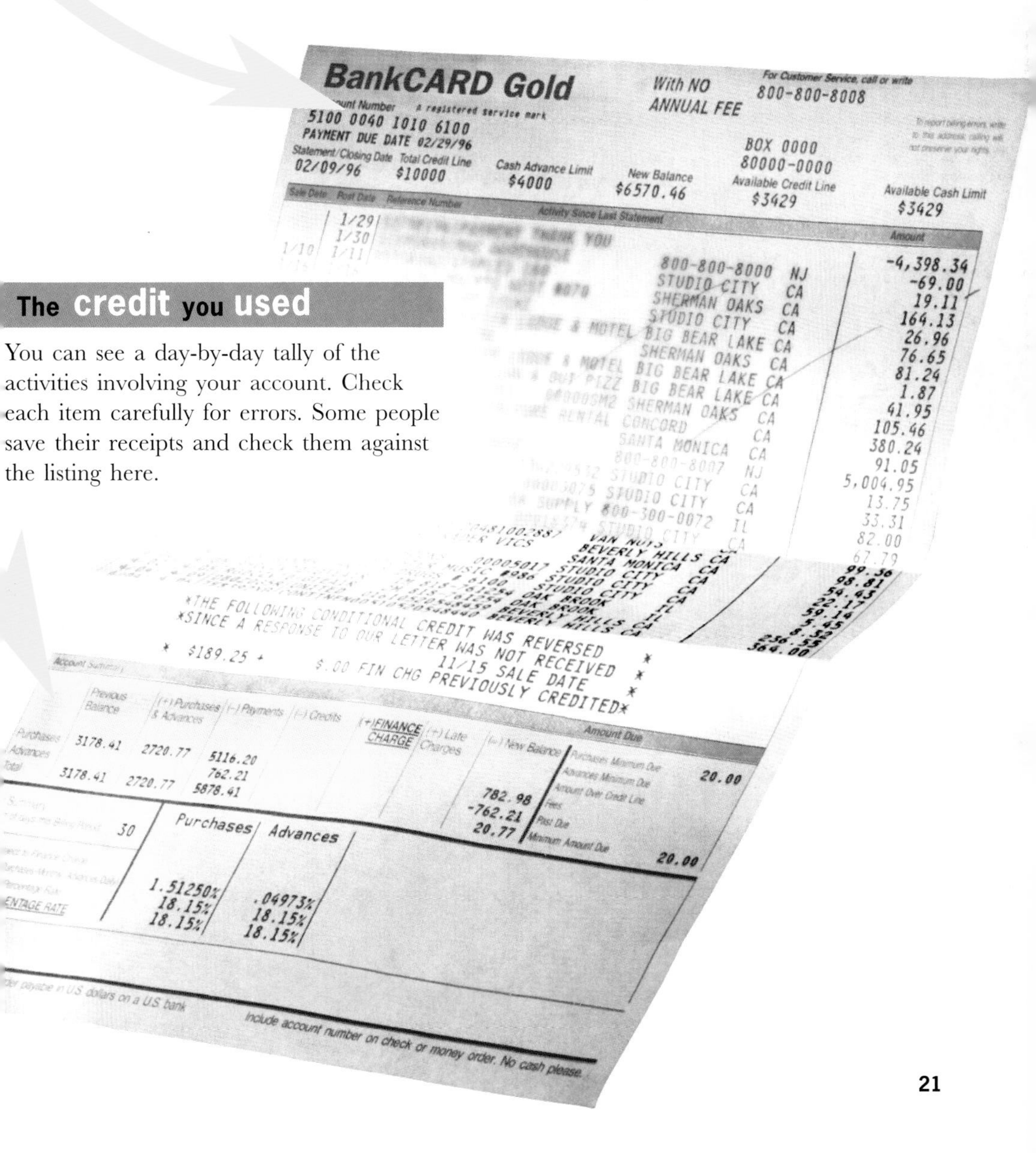

The credit you used

You can see a day-by-day tally of the activities involving your account. Check each item carefully for errors. Some people save their receipts and check them against the listing here.

Knowing your card rights

The Fair Credit Billing Act protects you from both honest errors and outright fraud by merchants when you buy something using a credit or travel and entertainment (charge) card. You don't receive as much protection, though, when using debit cards, such as an ATM card, that take money directly from your bank account.

Three of the most important safeguards are against:

Billing errors

If you find what you think is an error on your statement, you can withhold payment on the amount (or ask for a credit if you've already paid) while the card issuer investigates the problem. You must notify the customer service department (not the department where you send your bills) in writing within 60 days of the billing date (also called the closing date). A phone call won't protect your rights. The billing date appears on the front of each statement.

Once notified, the card issuer has up to 30 days to respond to you and up to 90 days to resolve the problem. If there's no resolution within 90 days, you can deduct $50 from the amount even if you lose the dispute. Include any evidence, such as receipts, that support your claim.

Defects or disputes

By law, every product must work properly if used for its intended purpose. When you use a card, you get "buyer protection" help against charges that are:

- above the agreed-upon price
- for items ordered but never sent
- for merchandise you didn't order
- for things that don't work as they're supposed to
- for unsatisfactory services

First, you must try to resolve the issue directly with the seller. If that doesn't work, you can refuse to pay the bill and ask the card issuer to step in. The card issuer must try to resolve the problem within 90 days. If it takes longer, you may not be liable for the charge at all.

Buyer protection applies to purchases over $50 made in your home state or within 100 miles of your mailing address. (If the card issuer is connected to the product, there are no restrictions.)

The effect of disputes on your credit

During a dispute, the card issuer isn't permitted to report the amount to a credit bureau as a delinquent payment, and no collection agency can come after you. The issuer can continue to tally interest charges against the amount (in case you end up owing it), and they can apply the amount to your credit limit.

If the situation isn't settled to your satisfaction, you can notify the issuer in writing within 10 days. That will give you extra protection, because if they report it as a non payment, they'll be required to report your side of the story as well.

No to annual fee. Card issuers are legally required to show the annual fee on the statement in the period before it's due, so you can decide whether you want to pay it. If you decide not to pay, you're asked to cut up the card and return it. You can still use the card until the end of the billing period. The issuer will continue to bill you monthly until you repay what you owe.

Unauthorized use of the card

Once you report a card lost or stolen, you're not liable for any purchases or cash advances made without your consent. In any event, as long as you report the card missing within a reasonable time (e.g., 30 days), you're only liable for up to $50. The phone number to call to report a lost or stolen card is on the back of every statement.

Many card issuers offer a lost or stolen card protection service for a fee (typically between $15 and $45 a year). When considering whether this service is worth the fee, keep in mind your liability is limited by law to $50 anyway, as long as you call your card issuer quickly.

Card blocks. Some hotels put a "block" on your credit card for an amount they estimate you'll spend during your stay. (Some car rental companies do the same.) Then they sometimes don't release the funds until weeks later. If you don't discover the block, you could be at a store and have your credit refused because you're at your credit limit. You have the right, however, to insist that a block be lifted when you check out of a hotel or return a car.

ATM cards are different. You have 60 days from the date on your statement to report a billing error. Here's the law for reporting lost or stolen cards: If you notify the bank within 2 business days, you're liable for up to $50. If you notify them within 60 days, you're liable for up to $500. After that, your liability is unlimited—until you report the card stolen.

How card payments work

Card issuers explain their methods for calculating finance charges (interest) on the back of each statement. The most common method is "average daily balance." To calculate this balance, the issuer totals what you owed at the end of each day in the billing period, and then divides that amount by the number of days in the period. That reveals the average amount you owed at the end of a day during that period,

and determines the interest charged.

Here's a comparison

By making a large purchase at the start of a billing period instead of at the end, you end up paying more in interest. Notice how the average daily balance rises, even without new purchases, because there are more days with the higher balance outweighing the days with the lower balance.

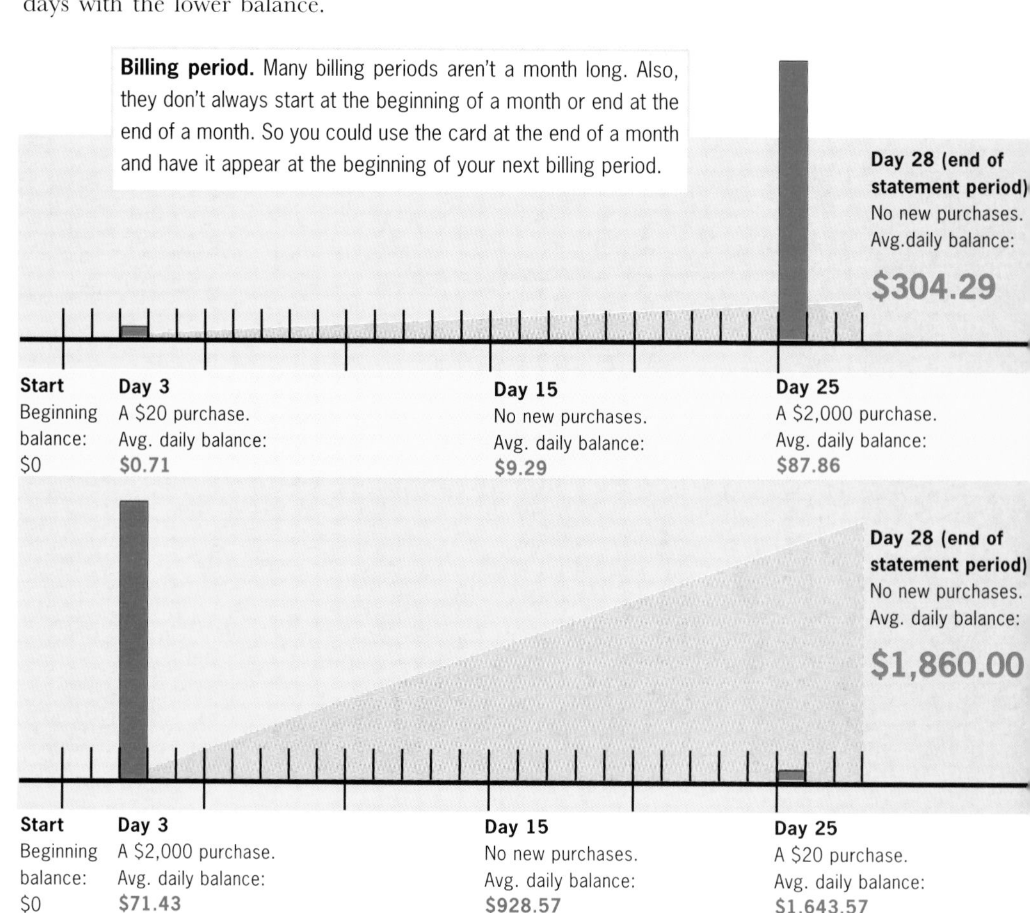

How much goes to pay interest. This example keeps the same minimum payment for the entire payment period (for simplicity's sake). So, while not entirely accurate, it provides a sense of how much you'd pay in interest by making only minimum payments on a $1,000 credit card purchase. In this case, it would take you 43 months to repay in full and cost $360 in interest.

Month	Payment	Interest portion	Total interest	Balance owed
1	$32	$15	$15	$983
5	32	14	72	912
10	32	13	138	818
15	32	11	196	716
30	32	6	322	362
40	32	2	357	77
43	32	0	360	0

Teaser rates. Many card offers promote low introductory rates. When the introductory period ends, the card issuer will automatically begin charging the higher interest rate on any balance you carry at the time.

Can you do better? Many experts say card issuers are often willing to negotiate the annual fee and even the finance charge, particularly for good customers.

Grace period. Some issuers give you time (a grace period) from the end of the billing cycle to pay your bill (commonly 20 or 25 days). If you start the billing cycle with a $0 balance and pay in full by the due date, you'll pay no interest. The moment you carry over a balance to the next period, the issuer will immediately charge interest on every purchase.

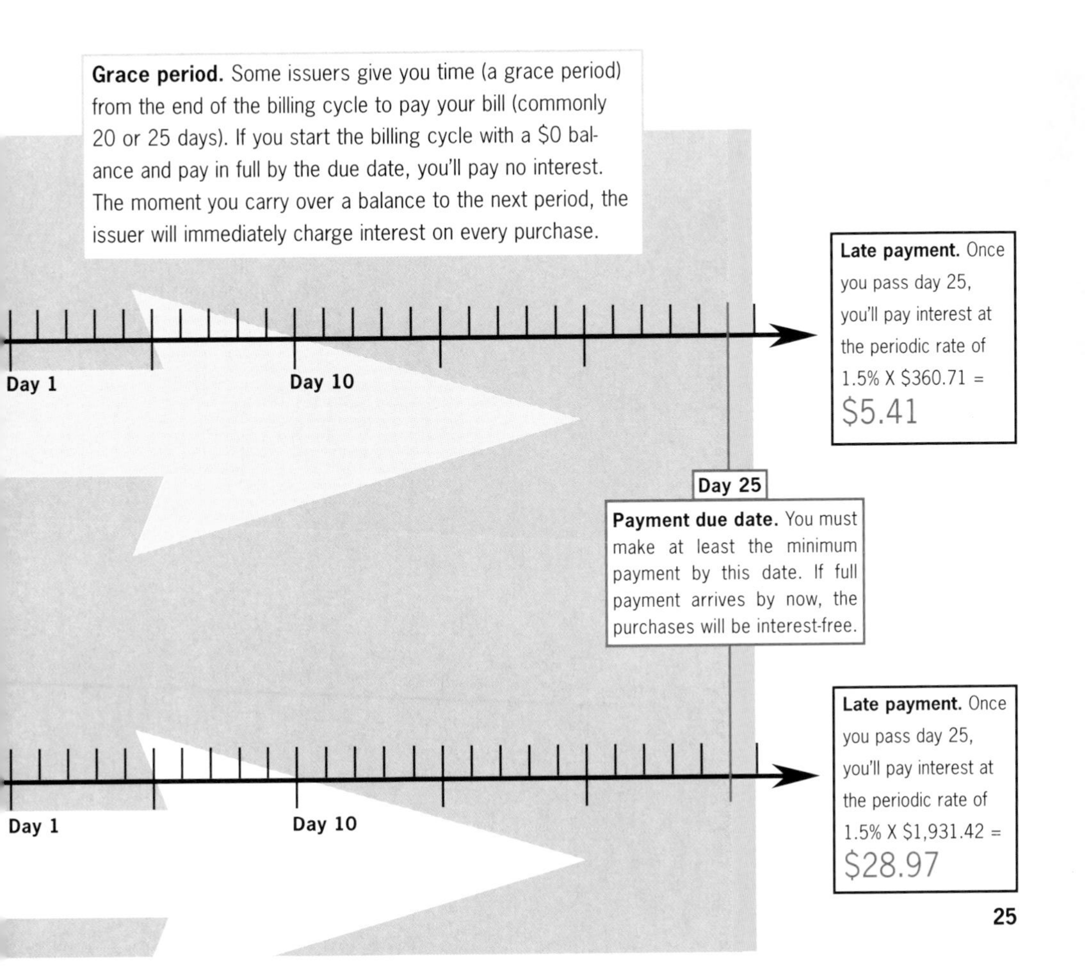

Late payment. Once you pass day 25, you'll pay interest at the periodic rate of 1.5% X $360.71 = $5.41

Payment due date. You must make at least the minimum payment by this date. If full payment arrives by now, the purchases will be interest-free.

Late payment. Once you pass day 25, you'll pay interest at the periodic rate of 1.5% X $1,931.42 = $28.97

Using what you've got to get more

To a lender, the most attractive borrower is someone with assets under the lender's control. If you have proven financial responsibility, you're even more attractive. With these two advantages, you can often get a loan more quickly and at better terms

by leveraging the power of your assets.

Your home

One of the most common—and most tempting—resources for a loan is your home's equity (the difference between what you owe and what the home is worth). Many lenders look for at least a 30% difference. In exchange for the loan, you'll give the lender a secondary interest in your home. (Your original mortgage lender has first interest.) If you fail to make your home equity loan payments, the lender can force the sale of the home but won't receive any proceeds until the lender of the first mortgage is paid in full.

There are two kinds of home equity loans: A "second mortgage" is a lump sum that you repay in scheduled installments. There's also a "home equity line of credit" where you can borrow any amount up to the limit, at any time, for any reason. You then repay it the same way you repay your credit cards.

Your securities

Brokerage firms lend money "on margin." The most they'll lend is a percentage of the total value of the "marginable" securities in your account (the ones the broker considers valuable enough to protect the firm if you default). The broker gives you the loan and you give the broker the right to sell the securities in your account if you fail to repay. You pay interest on the loan and repay it as you would any other.

The attraction of margin loans is the interest rate: It is usually a few points less than you'd pay at a bank. Margin loans can be risky, however. If the prices of your marginable securities drop to a point where their value doesn't leave enough protection, the broker will make a "margin call" (ask you to put in more money or pledge more securities). Failure to meet a margin call means instant sale of the securities you've already pledged—often at a loss.

Your life insurance

If you have a whole life policy (not term insurance), you may be able to borrow an amount equal to its "cash surrender value." This is exactly what it says: the amount of cash you'll receive if you decide to stop paying premiums and surrender the policy. The longer you own the policy (and the more premiums you pay), the more the cash surrender value increases.

The interest charged on such a loan varies from company to company. Often, though, it's lower than a bank loan. An insurance company also isn't as concerned about being repaid so long as you make the interest payments on schedule. If you die before the loan is repaid, they'll simply deduct what's owed to them and then pay out the remaining value of the policy.

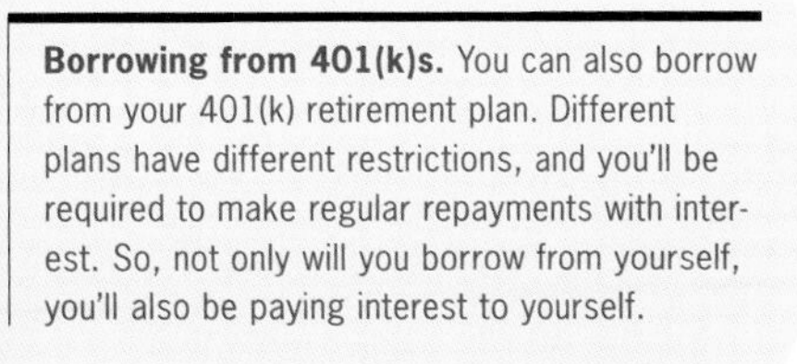

Borrowing from 401(k)s. You can also borrow from your 401(k) retirement plan. Different plans have different restrictions, and you'll be required to make regular repayments with interest. So, not only will you borrow from yourself, you'll also be paying interest to yourself.

Buyer beware

The credit world is ripe for unscrupulous people because so many credit transactions are conducted over the phone and through the use of

unfair, misleading, or illegal practices.

Preapproval/Guaranteed approval

Some ads guarantee you'll be approved for a card no matter what your credit history or how much you deposit in a special account. These should be reported to your state's consumer protection agency. Also, be suspicious of people who want a fee for getting you a card. You could do it yourself.

Another caution: Some guarantees end up being approvals for a tiny credit limit (e.g., $100). The issuer then checks your credit profile and, if it shows problems, refuses to raise your limit.

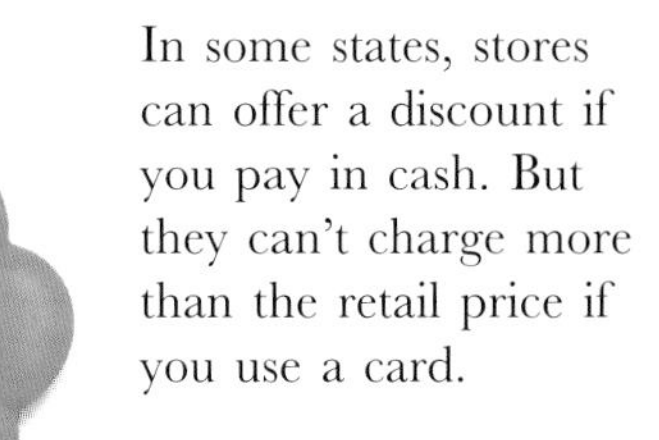

Don't write, don't phone

Many businesses want your address or phone number for their mailing lists, or to sell to a direct mail company. Most card issuers, however, forbid this practice. Also, in many states it's illegal for stores to write your credit card number on your check. Some experts recommend you don't let anyone write down your driver's license number if it's also your social security number.

Minimums and discounts

This isn't unfair, misleading, or illegal, but it's valuable to know: MasterCard and Visa don't let stores require minimum purchases. American Express follows the same policy if the store also takes Visa or MasterCard. Discover does permit it.

In some states, stores can offer a discount if you pay in cash. But they can't charge more than the retail price if you use a card.

Where to complain

If you think a store has been unfair, you can report them to your state or city consumer protection office or attorney general. Diners Club and American Express want to know about violations of their rules. For problems with Visa or MasterCard, start with a call to the bank that issued your card; if there's no satisfaction, try Visa or MasterCard themselves.

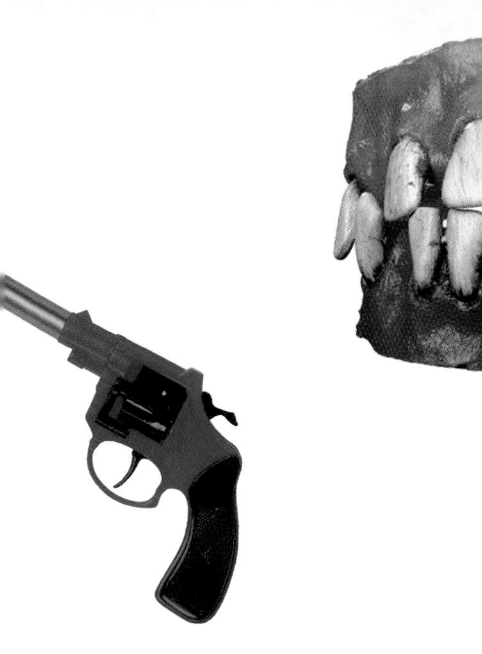

Phone calls

Experts say that people who call and ask for your credit card number or send a postcard and ask you to respond are probably scamming you, even if they sound legitimate.

Close but no cigar

Some ads offer cards that look a lot like a Visa or MasterCard but are merely gold-colored cards you can use only to shop through a specific catalogue—often at higher prices. Look for the Visa or MasterCard logo to be sure of what's offered.

Credit consultants

Some people calling themselves consultants or credit repair experts charge a lot to do what you could easily do yourself or what shouldn't be done at all. For example, they may dispute accurate items on your credit report to see if they can find a way to have the items removed. Their disputes could end up causing you more trouble instead of less, and cost high fees.

Special fees

Some card issuers charge a fee every time you check your balance or request other information through their toll-free customer service phone line. Ask about special fees when applying.

Contests and promotions

There are many scams (and legal but misleading marketing campaigns) that "guarantee" you've won a prize "with no obligation to buy," or offer "tremendous discounts" if you call right away. These people are usually either trying to get your credit card number so they can use it or slowly lure you into using your card to buy their product (at an inflated price and which you may never receive). This is a big problem area for law enforcement and consumers. The offers seem so tempting that people want to believe they'll win something for free, despite their better judgment.

Application information

By federal law, anyone offering a card must display a table with certain basic information, including the annual percentage rate (APR), annual fee, and grace period. If you can't find it, be suspicious.

Fraud victim assistance. Trans Union has a department dedicated to investigating potential frauds. If you think you've been a victim, call 1-800-680-7289.

Handling too much debt

Sometimes we just can't get out of debt. Situations beyond our control can arise and overwhelm us. Uninsured medical bills, a loss of business, or unemployment can happen to anyone. The natural reaction may be to cover your head and hide, but you'll usually be offered help if you genuinely try to remedy the situation.

There are three options:

Talk directly with creditors

The people to whom you owe money (your creditors) are motivated by two needs: to be repaid and to keep you as a customer. This tends to work in your favor.

Legally, as soon as you default on a debt (e.g., make a late payment), the creditor has the right to ask you to repay the entire debt. That rarely happens because the creditor is interested in building a relationship with you and selling more products or services. Most creditors, therefore, will listen if you ask for help in structuring a new repayment plan. For example, they may grant an extension of time or reduce payment amounts (and increase the number of payments).

If you're late paying, creditors typically send you form letters as polite reminders. If you still don't pay, they send letters with increasing intensity, or they call you on the phone. Eventually, a creditor will make demands, backed by the threat of action (such as a lawsuit or collection process).

Get outside help

If you can't work directly with a creditor, you could enlist help from:

A local credit counseling service. Find a service that is associated with the Consumer Credit Counseling Service (CCCS), a non profit organization supported partly by the credit industry. For a small fee, a counselor acts as a go-between with your creditors and helps set up a workable repayment plan.

Mediation. Becoming more popular is the use of a neutral third party to help you and the creditor open a line of communication and resolve your own dispute. It's very informal; the mediator can't force either side to do anything.

Arbitration. You and the creditor can agree to argue before a neutral third party (often a lawyer or judge). If it's not for a lot of money, the process is informal and probably doesn't require a lawyer. Both you and the creditor are bound by the decision (and the winner may also win a refund of the arbitration fee).

Debt consolidation. Debt consolidators—businesses that charge a fee to combine your debts and help you manage paying them off—are prohibited in most states and regulated in others. Apparently, most of these businesses are really looking to find ways to charge you high interest and fees. Non profit organizations are exempt from these state laws.

Deal with bill collectors

The last resort of any creditor, other than suing you (which may not be economically feasible), is to hand over your debt to a collection agency. These people aren't interested in keeping you as a customer. They're paid for results and have one goal: to recoup as much debt as they can.

Help from the government. If you feel you're being treated unfairly, you can invoke your rights by contacting the Federal Trade Commission (202-326-2222). It always helps to have a witness or some documented proof to verify your claim.

Your rights. Bill collectors are restricted by the Fair Debt Collection Practices Act, which applies to everyone who collects consumer debt for someone else, including attorneys. Here are some laws:

- You have the right to tell collectors not to contact you again. After that they can only call to say collection efforts have ended or that you're going to be sued.
- They can't threaten violence or use obscene or profane language.
- They can't contact you at work, and they can only call you at home between 8 am and 9 pm. Even then, they can't pester you on the phone.
- They can't put any markings on the outside of a letter or postcard that would reveal they're trying to collect a debt.
- They can't mislead you into repaying a debt.

Bankruptcy

Your creditors will be more interested in finding a way to get back their money than in forcing you into bankruptcy. But bankruptcy is an acceptable legal process that seeks the best resolution for you and your creditors. Although it's preferable to avoid the intrusion, stigma, and future credit problems that bankruptcy brings, sometimes it's the best solution. Once you apply to the courts, all collection efforts against you must stop, you're not allowed to take on new debts, and your assets are frozen.

You have two options:

Ask for a plan

You can apply for Chapter 7 bankruptcy. Here, you ask the court to create a workable plan and to carry it out. Your assets are frozen and a court-appointed person ("trustee") takes control of your finances. The trustee's job is to analyze your assets, income, and debts, then create the plan to distribute your assets to creditors as fairly as possible and in an orderly manner.

Usually, you'll be allowed to keep a certain amount of "exempt" assets in order to maintain a reasonable, modest lifestyle. Your income is usually protected so you can continue to support your family.

Once your assets have been distributed, the balance of your debts will be forgiven—except for certain obligations, such as child support, alimony, and criminal liability. So, depending on your circumstances, you could be debt-free; although you'll have a damaged credit record that will take time to rebuild.

Secured loans. Creditors with secured loans (loans for which you've specifically pledged your home, car, or other property) are first in line to be repaid from the sale of that property.

The process

1. Good professional guidance is advisable, but there are also self-filing forms available from books or the local court. (Filing fees are around $200.) You may file for Chapter 7 only every six years. There's no limit on filing for Chapter 13.
2. You'll be asked to provide verification of:
   - income and property owned
   - debts
   - monthly living expenses
   - property you're claiming as exempt

What's protected, what's not. Some debts are dischargeable (they'll be forgiven even if you don't repay in full). Some assets are exempt (they can't be used to repay debt). Here are some examples of dischargeable and exempt assets in some states; be sure to consult an attorney.

DEBTS		ASSETS	
Dischargeable	**Cannot be discharged**	**Exempt**	**Not exempt**
back rent, utility bills, personal loans, legal or accounting fees, court judgments	alimony, credit card charges, child support, tax obligations, student loans, medical bills, fines	your main car, tools of your trade, food, clothes, family heirlooms	luxury items, limited personal property, investments, cash

Create your own plan

Applying for Chapter 13 protection is similar to Chapter 7, but gives you more flexibility to resolve your debts as you see fit.

After filing, you present the court with your own scheme to repay your creditors, usually within three to five years. Generally, you must pledge all your disposable income (what's left after reasonable living expenses) to the plan.

If the court accepts your plan, you'll make your payments to the court-appointed trustee, who will monitor your situation and distribute the money to your creditors. At the end of the process, you'll be allowed to keep your remaining property, and the balance of any debts will be wiped out (unless, by law, they can't be discharged).

If the court doesn't accept your plan, you may be able to submit another plan or switch to Chapter 7.

Fraud warning. Some people try to use courts to avoid debts. If you've transferred property, withdrawn lots of cash, or bought luxury items immediately prior to filing, a court will investigate the possibility of fraud.

3. After you've filed, you'll attend a "creditors' meeting." Here, creditors can state their cases before the trustee, who then decides what's to be done. Since there usually isn't enough money for everyone, creditors accept a fraction of what they're owed.

4. A bankruptcy stays on your credit report for 10 years. When you begin applying for credit again, some lenders—but not all—will consider you too great a risk. By using tools such as secured credit cards, you can gradually rebuild a positive credit profile.

Who's who

The Federal Trade Commission (FTC)

This is the federal agency in charge of anything to do with credit (along with many other aspects of our economy). You can send them written complaints, particularly if you can't resolve a dispute with a credit bureau or card issuer. The national office is in Washington, D.C., and there are regional offices in Atlanta, Boston, Chicago, Cleveland, Dallas, Denver, Los Angeles, New York, San Francisco, and Seattle.

Creditors

These are the people to whom you owe money. A secured creditor is someone who extends you credit in return for your pledge that they can sell designated property of yours if you fail to repay the loan properly. An unsecured creditor is still entitled to be repaid somehow, but doesn't have the right to take and sell any specific property.

Credit guarantee company

When the store clerk runs your card through its machine, the clerk is contacting a credit guarantee company. This company, a liaison between the card issuer and the store, sends back the status of your credit to let the clerk know whether to make the sale, reject it, or even keep your card so you can't use it anymore.

Merchant banks and issuing banks

When you buy something using a card from Visa or MasterCard, the seller receives its payment from a "merchant" bank (minus a service fee that's typically 1% to 6% of your purchase). The merchant bank then is reimbursed by the "issuing" bank (minus a service fee that's typically 1% or 2%). The issuing bank is the one who issued you the card and the one who sends you a monthly statement requesting payment.

Visa and MasterCard

These competing organizations don't issue credit cards. They provide operational and marketing support for the banks who issue their cards. The banks are allowed to set their own credit terms, including the interest rate, grace period, and annual fee, as long as they stay within the guidelines of their member organization. Beside generating income from consumers, Visa and MasterCard also charge merchants a percentage of each purchase made with their card.

[Appendix]

GOVERNMENT HELP

If you feel you're being unfairly treated, you can invoke your rights by contacting the Federal Trade Commission (202-326-2222), or you can contact your state agency. It always helps to have a witness or some documented proof to verify your claim.

Alabama
Consumer Assistance, Office of Attorney General, Montgomery.
(334) 242-7334
(800) 392-5658

Alaska
Office of Attorney General, Juneau.
(907) 465-3600

Arizona
Consumer Information and Complaints, Office of Attorney General, Phoenix.
(602) 542-5763
(800) 352-8431

California
Department of Consumer Affairs, Sacramento.
(916) 445-1254
(800) 952-5210

Colorado
Consumer Protection Unit, Office of Attorney General, Denver.
(303) 866-5189
(800) 332-2071

Connecticut
Department of Consumer Protection, Hartford.
(860) 566-1543
(800) 842-2649

Delaware
Department of Justice, Consumer Protection Unit, Wilmington.
(302) 577-3250

District of Columbia
Department of Consumer and Regulatory Affairs, Washington, D.C.
(202) 727-7000
(800) 766-0122

Florida
Division of Consumer Services, Department of Agriculture and Consumer Services, Tallahassee.
(904) 922-2966
(800) 435-7352

Georgia
Governor's Office of Consumer Affairs, Atlanta.
(404) 651-8600

Hawaii
Office of Consumer Protection, Department of Commerce and Consumer Affairs, Honolulu.
(808) 586-2630

Idaho
Consumer Protection Division, Office of Attorney General, Boise.
(208) 334-2424
(800) 432-3545

Illinois
Consumer Protection Division, Office of Attorney General, Springfield.
(217) 782-9011
(800) 252-8666

Indiana
Consumer Protection Division, Office of Attorney General, Indianapolis.
(317) 232-6330
(800) 382-5516

Iowa
Consumer Protection Division, Office of Attorney General, Des Moines.
(515) 281-5926

Kansas
Consumer Protection Division, Office of Attorney General, Topeka.
(913) 296-3751
(800) 432-2310

Kentucky
Consumer Protection Division, Office of Attorney General, Frankfort.
(502) 573-2200

Louisiana
Consumer Protection Section, Office of Attorney General, Baton Rouge.
(504) 342-9638
(800) 351-4889

Maine
Bureau of Consumer Protection, Augusta.
(207) 624-8527
(800) 332-8529

Maryland
Consumer Protection Division, Office of Attorney General, Baltimore.
(410) 528-8662

Massachusetts
Consumer Protection Department, Office of Attorney General, Boston.
(617) 727-8400

Michigan
Consumer Protection Division, Office of Attorney General, Lansing.
(517) 373-1140

Minnesota
Citizen Assistance Center, Office of Attorney General,
(612) 296-3353
(800) 657-3787

Mississippi
Consumer Protection Division, Office of Attorney General, Jackson.
(601) 359-4230
(800) 281 4418

Missouri
Consumer Protection Division, Office of Attorney General, Jefferson City.
(314) 751-3321
(800) 392-8222

Montana
Consumer Affairs Unit, Department of Commerce, Helena.
(406) 444-4312

New Mexico
Consumer Protection Division, Office of Attorney General, Santa Fe.
(505) 827-6060
(800) 678-1508

New York
Consumer Protection Board, Albany.
(518) 474-8583

N. Carolina
Consumer Protection Section, Office of Attorney General, Raleigh.
(919) 733-7741

N. Dakota
Consumer Protection Division, Office of Attorney General, Bismarck.
(701) 328-3404
(800) 472 2600

Nebraska
Consumer Protection Division, Office of Attorney General, Lincoln.
(402) 471-2682

Nevada
Consumer Affairs Division, Las Vegas.
(702) 486-7355

New Hampshire
Consumer Protection Bureau Department of Justice, Concord.
(603) 271-3641

New Jersey
Division of Consumer Affairs, Newark.
(201) 504-6200

Ohio
Consumer Protection Division, Office of Attorney General, Columbus.
(614) 466-4986
(800) 282-0515

Oklahoma
Consumer Affairs Division, Office of Attorney General, Oklahoma City.
(405) 521-4274

Oregon
Financial Fraud, Department of Justice, Salem.
(503) 378-4320

Pennsylvania
Bureau of Consumer Protection, Office of Attorney General, Harrisburg.
(717) 787-9707
(800) 441-2555

Rhode Island
Consumer Protection Division, Office of Attorney General, Providence.
(401) 277-2104

S. Carolina
Department of Consumer Affairs, Columbia.
(803) 734-9452
(800) 922-1594

S. Dakota
Division of Consumer Protection, Office of Attorney General, Pierre.
(605) 773-4400
(800) 300-1986

Tennessee
Division of Consumer Affairs, Department of Commerce and Insurance, Nashville.
(615) 741-4737
(800) 342-8385

Texas
Consumer Protection Division, Office of Attorney General, Austin.
(512) 463-2070

Utah
Division of Consumer Protection, Department of Business Regulation, Salt Lake City.
(801) 530-6601
(800) 721-7233

Vermont
Consumer Assistance, Office of Attorney General, Burlington
(802) 656-3183
(800) 649-2424

Virginia
Office of Consumer Affairs, Department of Agriculture and Consumer Services, Richmond.
(804) 786-2042

Washington
Consumer Resource Center, Office of Attorney General, Seattle.
(206) 464-6684
(800) 551-4636

W. Virginia
Consumer Protection Division, Office of Attorney General, Charleston.
(304) 558-8986
(800) 368-8808

Wisconsin
Department of Agriculture, Trade and Consumer Protection, Madison.
(608) 224-4953
(800) 422-7128

Wyoming
Consumer Affairs Division, Office of Attorney General, Cheyenne
(307) 777-7874
(800) 438-5799

Here's an example of an unsolicited credit approval. The lender sends a check in the mail and gives a recipient the immediate ability to cash it—which makes it very tempting. Because it's designed as a check, this loan almost feels like free money (just cash the check and the money is yours). Recipients who read the rest of the solicitation, however, would see that cashing the check automatically obligates them to repay a loan at a very high interest rate (as shown by the box inset below).

139993 14-65/55500

Date: 04/08/96

Amount:
$5,000.00

Five Thousand Dollars and no cents

Pay to the order of

JOHN DOE
123 FIRST STREET
ANYTOWN, USA 99504-0000

Not valid for an amount over $5,000. Check not valid after 45 days from date above. Payee's endorsement required.

By ______________
Senior Vice President

0528 0469 02/96 CA 2044

⑈110011⑈ ⑆122000001⑆ 11008⑈00098⑈

DETACH HERE

SIMPLY USE THIS CHECK ↑

JOHN DOE
The above guaranteed Loan Check for $5,000.00 is REAL!
Just cash it before the expiration date and the money is yours.

Dear JOHN DOE

You've been a valued customer, so here's a very special offer.

Enclosed is a check loan for $5,000.00—and it's real. All you have to do is cash it and the money is yours to use any way you see fit.

This is just our way of saying thank you for being a responsible borrower. Now you can use this cash to consolodate bills, take vacations, fix up your home or pay for school.

We hope you'll take advantage of this offer. Simply:

- endorse the guaranteed loan check and cash it by the expiration date.
- read the attached terms and conditions of your loan.

If you need more money, please call and let us know.

GUARANTEED LOAN CHECK FOR $5,000.00
Monthly Payment: $135.23
Annual Percentage Rate: 20.99%
Finance Charge: $3,113.80
Amount Financed: $5,0000
Total of Payments: $8,113.80
Number of Payments: 60
Contract Rate: 20.70%

LOAN DISCLOSURE

In most cases, lenders are required to give you a plain English explanation of the main terms of your loan. The required document, shown here, is called the Truth-In-Lending Disclosure Statement. The most important information to comprehend always appears along the top portion of the statement: the APR (which takes into account the interest plus fees), the finance charge (the amount you'll pay in interest over the life of the loan), the amount financed (the amount borrowed), and the total of payments (the total interest plus the repayment of what you borrowed). The remainder of the information is also very important: some of the main rights and responsibilities you accept along with the loan.

SAVING BANK

Federal Truth-In-Lending Disclosure Statement

DATE:
LOAN NO:
BORROWERS:

ANNUAL PERCENTAGE RATE The cost of your credit as a yearly rate.	FINANCE CHARGE The dollar amount the credit will cost you.	AMOUNT FINANCED The amount of credit provided to you or on your behalf	TOTAL of PAYMENTS The amount you will have paid after you have made all payments as scheduled.
7.49 %	$ 619,899.00	$ 368,810.16	$ 619,899.00

Your Payment Schedule will be:

Number of Payments	Amount of Payments: Varying From:	To: (If Applicable)	Payments are due Monthly Beginning:
12	1,765.28	.00	JUNE 1st, 1996
12	1,897.68	.00	JUNE 1st, 1997
12	2,040.01	.00	JUNE 1st, 1998
12	2,193.01	.00	JUNE 1st, 1999
12	2,357.49	.00	JUNE 1st, 2000
299	2,885.58	.00	JUNE 1st, 2001
1	2,879.10	.00	MAY 1st, 2026
	.00	.00	
	.00	.00	

Variable Rate: YOUR LOAN CONTAINS A VARIABLE-RATE FEATURE, DISCLOSURES ABOUT THE VARIABLE-RATE FEATURE WERE PROVIDED TO YOU EARLIER.

Itemization of the amount financed: $ 368,810.16
$ **Amount given to you directly.**
Amount paid to others on you behalf:
$ $ 368,810.16 **to:** TITLE COMPANY
OTHER PAYMENTS NOT PART OF AMOUNT FINANCED:
$
$
$
Prepaid Finance Charge: $ 3,189.84

Security: [X] You are giving a security interest in the property being purchased.
[ ] (Other) ____

Required Deposit: The Annual Percentage Rate does not take into account your required deposit. You are giving a security interest in the required deposit/pledge account.

Late Charge: If payment is 15 Days late, you will be charged 5.00 % of payment.

Prepayment: If you pay off early, you
[X] may [ ] will not have to pay a penalty.
[ ] may [X] will not be entitled to a refund of part of the finance charge.

Assumption: Someone buying your home
[ ] cannot assume the remainder of the mortgage on the original terms.
[X] may, subject to conditions, be allowed to assume the remainder of the mortgage on the original terms.

Filling Fees: $ 52.00

Insurance: You may obtain property insurance from anyone you want that is acceptable to Lender.

See your contract documents for any additional information about non payment, default, any required repayment in full before the scheduled date, and prepayment refunds and penalties.

All numerical disclosures, except the late payment disclosure, are estimates.